THE TUTTLE TWINS
—— and the ——
MESSED UP
MARKET

Books in The Tuttle Twins series:

The Tuttle Twins Learn About the Law

The Tuttle Twins and the Miraculous Pencil

The Tuttle Twins and the Creature from Jekyll Island

The Tuttle Twins and the Food Truck Fiasco

The Tuttle Twins and the Road to Surfdom

The Tuttle Twins and the Golden Rule

The Tuttle Twins and the Search for Atlas

The Tuttle Twins and their Spectacular Show Business

The Tuttle Twins and the Fate of the Future

The Tuttle Twins and the Education Vacation

The Tuttle Twins and the Messed Up Market

Find them all at TuttleTwins.com

ISBN 978-1-943521-45-6

Boyack, Connor, author.
Stanfield, Elijah, illustrator.
The Tuttle Twins and the Messed Up Market / Connor Boyack.

Cover design by Elijah Stanfield
Edited and typeset by Connor Boyack

Printed in the United States

10 9 8 7 6 5 4 3

To Ludwig von Mises

For reminding us how
markets remain free.

Emily's nose was cold from the chilly spring breeze, but she was sweating under her jacket as she pedaled her bike ahead of Ethan, heading to the family theater for this week's building cleanup.

After a long winter it felt like this was the first time they had felt the sun's warmth for months.

The twins darted around orange cones that were redirecting traffic; the melting snow had caused some flooding along Main Street and cars were slowly being detoured down another road.

"Hot chocolate!" a boy shouted on a nearby corner. Many drivers were holding money out of their vehicle windows to buy a cup from the boy who was apparently doing quite well.

"Looks like he's doing better than our lemonade stand ever did," Ethan said to Emily, trying to catch his breath.

"Yeah, hot chocolate is a clever idea, especially with all this traffic going right by him," Emily replied. "We should stop and buy some. Besides, I could use a break."

The twins approached the boy who was a bit younger than them. He was clearly working hard to earn a lot of sales.

"Hi, I'm Maddox," the boy said with a slight lisp. "Can I get you a cup?"

"Two, please," Emily said. "This is quite a business you have going here."

Maddox flashed a gigantic grin, revealing some missing teeth. "When I looked out my window this morning I saw workers putting up cones on the street, so I knew people would be passing right by here. I also have a knack for selling people stuff," he bragged.

"My mom said the police might shut me down because I don't have some kind of permission slip, but no one has come yet," he added.

Emily handed Maddox a couple dollars, which he shoved into his already full pockets. He poured two steaming cups and then returned his attention to the line of potential customers driving by.

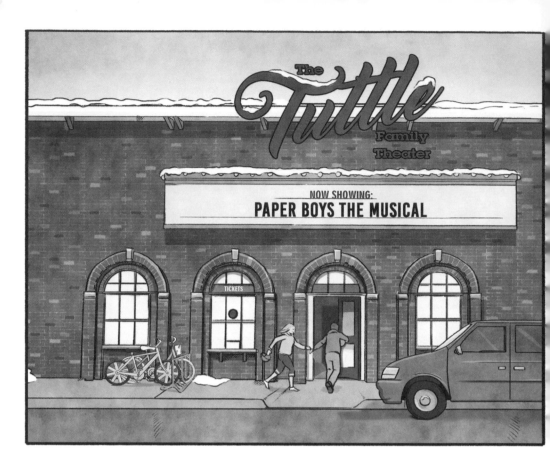

The twins arrived at the theater to find Nana waiting in the lobby with their parents, grinning even brighter than Maddox.

"Why are you all so happy?" Ethan asked.

"This, my young partners, is a business offer," Nana replied, holding out some papers. "Mrs. Dobson from the Tarp Troupe Theater wants to buy us out!"

"Our competition wants to buy our theater?" Ethan asked. "But we've been doing so well!"

"I'm sure that's exactly why she wants to buy!" Mrs. Tuttle chimed in.

"Before we decide, you should know..." Nana paused. "Each of you would receive $3,000 if we choose to sell. Also, you won't have to spend your weekends cleaning up the theater anymore."

"Those are strong *incentives* for kids your age!" Mr. Tuttle smiled, seeing their stunned expressions. "An incentive is something that motivates you to make a decision or to act. That much money and saving lots of time are good reasons to do the deal."

Nana explained that a decision like this has *trade-offs* to think about—positive and negative things that would happen depending on which course of action they decided to take.

"Both choices give us opportunities," Nana said, thinking out loud. "But when we choose one opportunity, we have to give up the other one. So that's the cost of trading one opportunity for another—the *opportunity cost*."

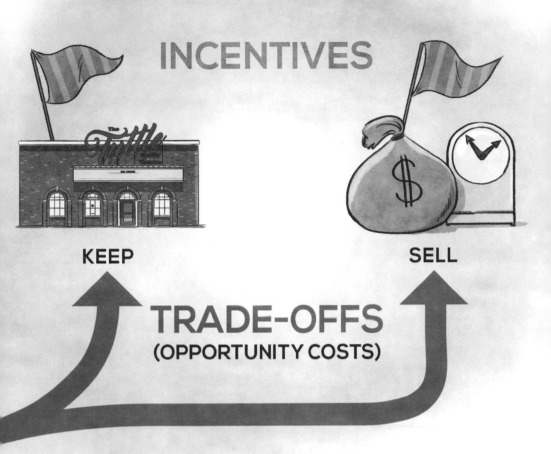

INCENTIVES

KEEP

SELL

TRADE-OFFS
(OPPORTUNITY COSTS)

"So are you incentivized to keep your theater business, hoping for more profit in the future?" Mrs. Tuttle asked. "That may take years of hard work."

"I think I have a greater incentive to get all that money now, and have fun on Saturdays again," Ethan said. "Selling seems like the trade-off that's best for me."

The twins looked at each other and then at Nana, each giving a slight nod. "Let's do it!" Emily said.

10

As was their tradition—and at Mr. Tuttle's suggestion—the family went out for ice cream that night to celebrate the sale of their company.

"I have so much money now," Emily said. "Maybe I should buy all the toys on my wish list!"

"That would be some serious instant gratification," Nana chuckled.

"What's wrong with being... gratified?" Ethan asked. "I have a lot of ideas for what to buy, too."

"Well, good things come to those who wait," Mrs. Tuttle said. "*Delayed gratification* is a powerful idea... making a choice to limit what you get now, so you can get something bigger or better later. It's a trade-off, just like we talked about before."

"When you two are older you will want other things—more expensive things—than a bunch of toys," Nana explained. "Maybe you should put that money in a savings account at the bank."

"Banks actually pay people who save money," Mr. Tuttle explained, "which they get from loaning that money out to others and charging them a fee, called *interest*. When we grew up, banks would charge a higher interest—that created an incentive for people to save more and borrow less."

"But these days you hardly get any interest for saving because the interest rate is very low," Mrs. Tuttle added. "Low interest creates an incentive to borrow money, since loans are cheap, and not save, since you get paid hardly anything."

"So if we save now we'll only earn a little interest?" Emily asked.

"It's worse," Mrs. Tuttle said. "Your money would lose value in a bank because the Federal Reserve keeps making new money. You'd get a little interest while inflation makes your money's value go down."

"The Creature from Jekyll Island strikes again!" Emily said. "It seems it's better to buy stuff now while the money is worth more."

13

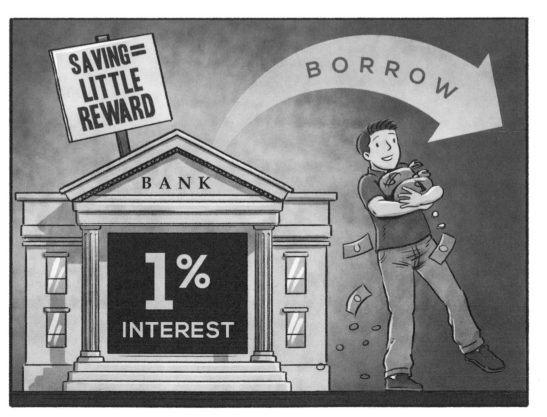

Ethan thought for a moment. "Banks don't save money... they loan it out to others, right? What if we did that too—charging interest for loans, just like a bank?"

The adults laughed, but suddenly stopped when they realized he was serious.

"But who would ask for a loan from a couple of kids?" Nana asked.

"Other kids!" the twins both answered—and that's when Mr. and Mrs. Tuttle realized that they were on to something.

"That's actually a really good idea," Mr. Tuttle said. "It could be an excellent educational experience for kids, and banks don't usually give loans to kids your age. Small loans are often a huge help to *microenterprises*."

"What are those?" Emily asked.

"Well, an enterprise is a fancy word for a business," he replied. "A microenterprise is a really small business often involving only one or a few people. And that applies to pretty much every business run by kids."

"That word is a mouthful," Ethan said, with a mouth full of ice cream.

The twins had stayed up late talking about their new business idea and left the house early to find kids who wanted to start up their own microenterprises.

"Maddox! Heyyyyy Maaaaaaadox!" the twins shouted.

"This is where he was selling, so he must live in one of these apartments," Ethan said, reassuring his sister after a few minutes had passed.

After shouting so loud they thought someone might call the police, a window opened on the second story of a nearby apartment building. "You guys want more hot chocolate?" asked Maddox.

"Not today," Emily yelled back, "but we have an idea for you."

Ethan and Emily explained to Maddox about the sale of the theater, and how they wanted to use their money to help kids start businesses with small loans.

"But we need to find a lot more kids like you," Ethan said. "So here's our idea: why not create a marketplace for young entrepreneurs like us? We'll call it the Children's Entrepreneur Market."

"I bet adults would love spending money at something like that!" Maddox smiled. "And if your market does well, I'm going to need a bigger hot chocolate maker. So a loan sounds like a good idea to me!" he said.

Convincing Maddox's parents to allow him to take a loan wasn't too difficult. The twins explained that Maddox would feel more accountable by borrowing from them, rather than using money from his parents, which is better practice for the real world. They signed a simple contract for a $200 loan, with $20 to be paid back as interest.

Weeks later, the first market opened on a large, grassy field at a nearby church. A couple dozen families showed up to participate. The sun was warm and people were excited because it was a new opportunity for children to make some money and learn about business.

To attract more customers and create incentives for young entrepreneurs to participate, the twins had spent some of their money on a marketing campaign with social media, newspaper ads, and posters around town. They planned to make the money back by charging each seller a small fee to participate in the market.

Maddox was busy at his booth. The new machine he had purchased with his loan allowed him to quickly make much more hot chocolate than he previously could.

"At this rate he'll be able to pay us back pretty quickly," Ethan said, watching nearby.

"I wish everyone here would take a loan from us!" Emily said, thinking about how easy it might be to earn extra money—without doing any extra work!

"But..." Mr. Tuttle replied, "what would happen if other kids aren't as successful as Maddox, and can't pay you back as fast—or at all? Are you prepared to take on that *risk* and potentially lose some of your hard-earned money?"

"How do we figure out how to make good loans that aren't risky?" Ethan wondered out loud, trying to think of an answer to his own question.

"Understanding people and their behavior helps," Mrs. Tuttle replied. "That's called praxeology!"

"Praxa-what?" Emily asked, clearly confused.

"*Praxeology* is the study of why humans act the way they do," Mr. Tuttle said, motioning to the twins to follow him down the aisle of booths. "Using this information you can better decide which businesses might be a wise choice for a loan, or a risky one."

Maddox was making a lot of sales nearby, with a steady line of customers.

"Your friend Maddox was a hard worker before you loaned him anything," Mr. Tuttle said. "Why do you think that is?"

"He seems to like making people happy," Ethan responded, "but he also told me he's trying to earn money for a new bike."

"So that's his motivation—his incentive," Mr. Tuttle explained. "It's a reason for his actions and why he is making careful decisions and working hard."

"It was probably a wise decision to loan him money."

Nearby, two siblings had been selling hot dogs, but they were already packing up. The twins learned that their parents made them come to the market, and wouldn't let them go home and play video games until they sold all of their hot dogs.

"With a loan they could have sold more hot dogs and made more money, but I'm glad we didn't offer them one," Ethan said as they walked toward the next booth. "They probably wouldn't keep selling after today to earn enough to pay us back!"

"And yet," Mr. Tuttle said, "those kids still have their own incentives—they simply want to play their video games."

"If their incentive had been to give yummy food to customers and make money, they might have worked harder and started a successful business," Emily suggested. "Oh well."

"There's a lot of people waiting over there," Ethan said, noticing a girl painting portraits that were in high demand. "But she's already painting as fast as she can. How could a loan help her?"

"Good question," a voice behind them said. The twins spun around to find Mrs. Dobson, the new owner of their theater. "Customers have an incentive to get a painting, and she has an incentive to earn their money—so they have to agree on a fair trade. Maybe she could raise prices to slow the demand, or she could hire another artist to increase the supply of paintings. Either choice could make her business more profitable, but only she can choose which opportunity is best for her."

Ethan decided to give the girl a flyer, just in case. "You seem good at business," he told Mrs. Dobson. "Could you help us figure out which kids to give loans to?"

Mr. Tuttle returned to the information booth while Mrs. Dobson took the twins through the market to make some recommendations.

"There are a lot of opportunities for who you might give a loan to," Mrs. Dobson said. "How do you want to narrow them down?"

"Our dad suggested we should stay away from risky ones," Emily said. "We want to give loans to kids who are going to work hard and pay us back, so we get interest. Then we can—"

"Hi there!" a young girl said, interrupting Emily. "Can I interest you in my caramel apples?"

The twins were impressed with the selection—the plate of samples she held up had apple pieces with a variety of different toppings.

"You can buy one for $5 or five for $20," the young entrepreneur told them. "I'd love to have you as a customer!"

"You're very outgoing," Mrs. Dobson told her. "Why are you working so hard at the market today?"

"Well, I haven't sold very many so far," she said. "Maybe they're too expensive. But I really want to earn money to help pay for my dad's medicine. He's sick and it costs a lot of money, so I want to help."

"That's a really good incentive. I hope your business succeeds so you can help him," Mrs. Dobson said, purchasing 25 apples—earning the girl a $100 bill.

"Thank you so much!" the girl said, her lip quivering a bit as she put the apples into a box.

Ethan explained that they were offering loans to kids like her, and how a loan might help her have money to make a big sign or do some marketing to attract more customers.

After an hour with Mrs. Dobson, the twins had
given out several loans totaling over $750.

There was one more booth to visit—and it had a
steady stream of customers who were filling a large
bowl with money, while helping themselves to some
brownies for 25 cents each. A boy stood nearby,
looking almost bored, playing with a yo-yo.

"Maybe this is why those caramel apples aren't
selling well?" Emily whispered to Ethan. "People are
getting their sugar fix here for cheap—but this kid
doesn't even seem to be working hard!"

"Do you think he's even making a profit by selling them at that price?" Ethan replied.

The boy looked up and locked eyes with the twins, so they introduced themselves and handed him a flyer. "My brother and I are giving loans to kids who want to build their business," Emily explained.

"Why would I want to borrow your money when my parents pay for everything I need?" the boy shrugged. "And my parents don't make me pay any interest like you're charging. I'm not even sure they care if I pay them back."

They had given out some loans, but the twins ended on a sour note with the brownie boy as they returned to their booth with Mrs. Dobson.

They explained to their parents what had happened, and that the boy already had a loan from his parents.

"But that isn't a loan," Mr. Tuttle corrected him. "He's getting a *subsidy*—free money. The problem with subsidies is that it prevents people from understanding the consequences of their actions. It makes no difference to them whether they make wise choices or poor choices with the money. If a kid will always get more money from his parents, why worry?"

"So brownie boy doesn't have an incentive to work hard or improve his business," Mrs. Dobson added.

"It's also probably the reason why he's selling them for so little," Emily observed. "He doesn't have to pay anyone back, so he doesn't care if the price is too low."

"That seems like unfair competition," Ethan said. "People are filling up on subsidized brownies rather than trying that girl's awesome apples... now the market is all messed up!"

"Subsidies mess up and distort the real world market all the time," Mrs. Dobson said. "In fact, your Nana told me it happened with her dance studio."

The twins remembered Nana explaining that her studio failed because the government built a recreation center that offered dance classes, but they used taxes to subsidize it, so the prices were low and she couldn't compete fairly.

"That's right," Mrs. Tuttle said. "I was so sad when I couldn't take dance classes at my mom's studio

COMMUNITY
RECREATIONAL
CENTER

anymore. Subsidies distort the market in ways that can really hurt people."

"A free market requires people to compete fairly for customers by providing better things for lower prices," Mr. Tuttle commented.

"Subsidies distort that process because it causes people to make different choices than they would have if the market was fair—sort of like how many customers chose subsidized brownies over fairly priced caramel apples."

"The same thing happens in the energy, automobile, and farming industries," Mr. Tuttle explained. "Every time government interferes in the market with subsidies it takes opportunities from entrepreneurs to compete fairly and discover better ways of doing things for the right prices for customers."

"Here's another example," Mrs. Tuttle said. "The people who grow corn get big subsidies from the government, which leads them to produce more corn than is needed. That extra supply drives down the price, making it cheaper than other products that might be better. Now our food is filled with corn syrup instead of other sweeteners like sugar— another distorted market."

"Hey... now that you're in the banking business," Mrs. Dobson said, winking at the twins, "you should know that banks are one of the most subsidized businesses in the world."

SUBSIDIZED BUSINESSES

DISADVANTAGED COMPETITION

Mr. Tuttle nodded somberly. "Do you remember that with low interest rates, people stop saving and start taking big loans instead? Some people might use that money wisely, but others want instant gratification and buy things that they can't afford. Then they might owe more money than they can ever pay back."

"If our customers didn't pay back the loans we gave them, we'd run out of money and go out of business!" Ethan exclaimed.

"That's where the subsidies come in," Mr. Tuttle continued. "When the bank is sinking because too many loans go unpaid, the government often gives free money to the bank—it's often called a bailout because it's like saving a sinking boat."

"But if their mistakes get bailed out, then they don't have an incentive to be careful about risky loans," Mrs. Dobson said. "Just like brownie boy, the bank doesn't care about messing up the market as long as they can get a subsidy later on, right?"

"Hey, what's she doing?" Ethan suddenly said.

The caramel apple girl was pushing a wheelbarrow full of brownies back to her booth. Seeing a few spill out, the twins rushed to help.

"My dad gave me an idea..." she told the twins. "So I bought the rest of the brownies with the $100 I made earlier, and I will sell them for 50 cents each to make a profit. Then, when people buy a brownie, I will offer them discounted apples to take home and share with others!"

The twins watched in amazement as a line soon started to form at her booth, seeing the new sign she had made—advertising both cheap brownies and delicious apples.

"You see?" Mrs. Dobson said, approaching the booth. "Even with some subsidies making the market unfair, people who are incentivized to work hard can still adapt and overcome obstacles. That's just the way humans act."

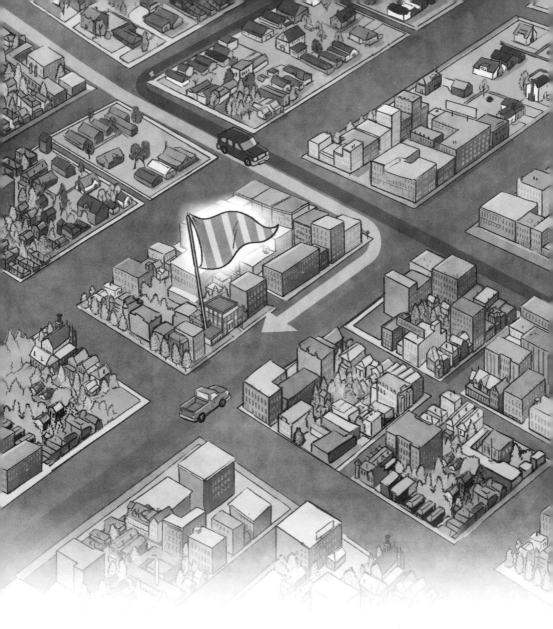

"Think of human action like traffic," Mrs. Dobson continued. "There are roads, signs, and rules that help drivers avoid crashing into each other or damaging property. People can move freely toward whatever destination they choose, as long as they don't hurt other people or break the basic rules."

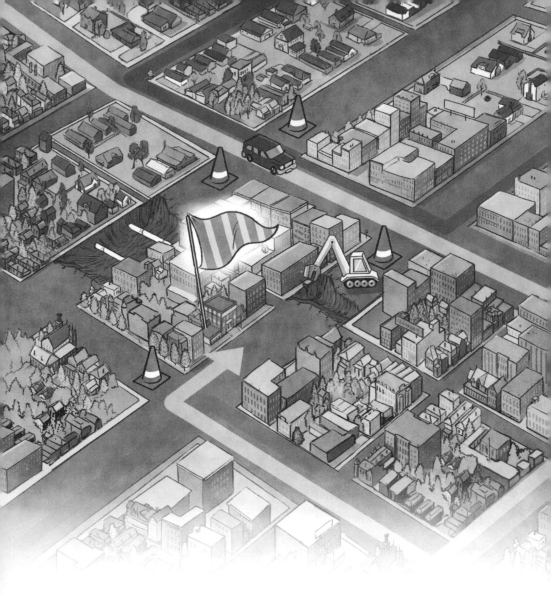

"But too often," she added, "government interferes—
so human action is forced in another direction.
The system gets distorted. People follow paths
they normally wouldn't take, and maybe make bad
choices about which way to go. Getting to their
destination becomes harder... but if they are willing
to keep at it, they'll usually find a way to get there."

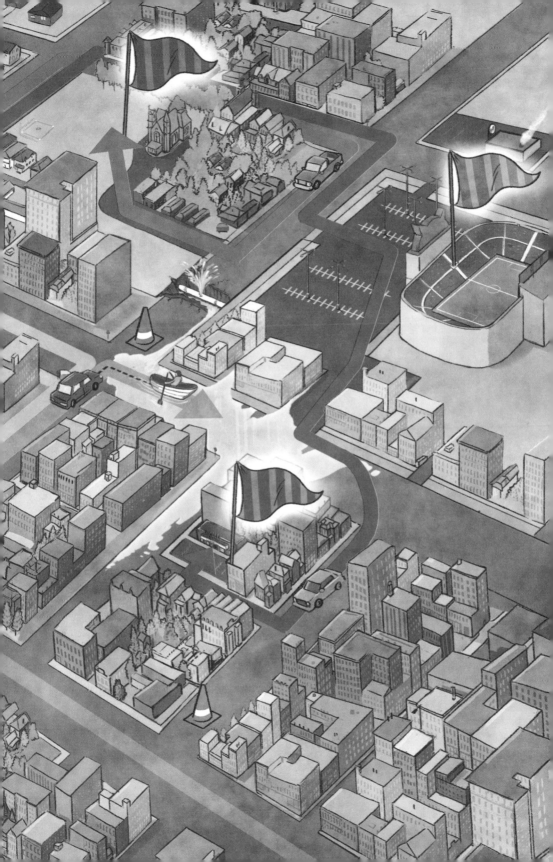

"It's the same with the government's distortions, if you—" She was cut off with the sound of a siren.

Police officers fanned out through the market while one person in a long coat—the new city manager—began speaking through a megaphone.

"Folks... children... I understand that you're all just peacefully buying and selling things, but..."

The "but" lingered in the air long enough for the twins to nervously wonder what was about to happen with their market.

"But doing business in this city requires compliance with our tax and regulatory codes," the man said. "None of you have permits so you're all in violation of the law. This market ends now."

Like a gigantic balloon slowly releasing its air, a unified groan came from the crowd. The sound of small, chilly rain drops pattered through the market as police officers hovered over the families packing up their booths.

"Hey mom," Emily said while lifting a heavy box, "I think our bank might need a bailout... we're not sure we will get paid back!"

"Nice try," Mrs. Tuttle replied. "You know better than that... bailouts aren't the Tuttle way."

"Seriously, how are we going to get our $750 back if these kids can't sell their stuff?" Ethan worried. "And what is that poor girl going to do with all those caramel apples and brownies?"

"She can sell more at your second Children's Entrepreneur Market!" Mrs. Dobson said, walking toward her car. "Remember, the best lessons we learn in life are from our failures and challenges. You're the vehicle going to your destination—this is just another obstacle you'll get around."

"We can start by getting that law changed so kids don't have to get all these silly permission slips," Mr. Tuttle suggested. "You did it once with food trucks, why not for microenterprises?"

Mr. Tuttle loaded the last of the boxes into the van as the police officers drove away.

"Cup of hot chocolate?" Maddox offered, approaching the Tuttle family. "It's on the house... I have a lot leftover. I even gave some to the police!"

"Oh, and here you go," he said, handing the twins the money he had borrowed, with interest. "I made so much today I can pay you back already!"

"But what about the bike you were wanting to save for?" Emily asked.

"You two seem to have enough money... want to just give me some?" Maddox joked.

"Tuttles don't give out subsidies," Ethan laughed. "But if you want another loan, let us know!"

The End

"Since nobody is in a position to substitute his own value judgments for those of the acting individual, it is vain to pass judgment on other people's aims and volitions. No man is qualified to declare what would make another man happier or less discontented."

—Ludwig von Mises

Among the great free market economists, Ludwig von Mises stands out prominently. A Jewish immigrant from Austria who came to the United States of America in 1940, he had foreseen years earlier the problems with national socialism in Germany and was a prolific professor highlighting why these problems would inevitably lead the country to ruin.

From his safer perch in America, Mises wrote a number of books, including *Human Action*—his "comprehensive treatise on economics" that explores why people make the decisions they do, and how this is connected to the workings of a free market economy.

Readers should note that this is an advanced book. For a simpler version, consider reading *Choice: Cooperation, Enterprise, and Human Action* by Robert Murphy.

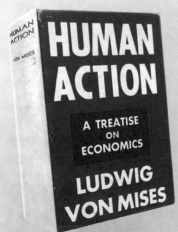

The Author

Connor Boyack is president of Libertas Institute, a free market think tank in Utah. In that capacity he has changed a significant number of laws in favor of personal freedom and free markets, and has launched a variety of educational projects, including The Tuttle Twins children's book series. Connor is the author of over a dozen books.

A California native and Brigham Young University graduate, Connor currently resides in Lehi, Utah, with his wife and two children.

The Illustrator

Elijah Stanfield is owner of Red House Motion Imaging, a media production company in Washington.

A longtime student of Austrian economics, history, and the classical liberal philosophy, Elijah has dedicated much of his time and energy to promoting the ideas of free markets and individual liberty. Some of his more notable works include producing eight videos in support of Ron Paul's 2012 presidential candidacy. He currently resides in Richland, Washington, with his wife April and their six children.

Contact us at TuttleTwins.com!

Glossary of Terms

Delayed Gratification: Resisting an immediate reward in favor of a later reward instead.

Incentive: Something that induces a person to action.

Interest: A fee charged to a person who borrows money.

Microenterprise: A small business employing only a few people.

Opportunity Cost: What a person misses out on by choosing an alternative option.

Praxeology: The study of human action.

Risk: The chance that something bad will be happen.

Subsidy: Monetary assistance, typically given with no expectation of repayment.

Trade-off: Reducing or losing one option in favor of increasing or gaining another.

Discussion Questions

1. Why don't banks just let people borrow money for free?
2. What is wrong with bailing out people who made poor choices?
3. Are there things for which you seek instant gratification?
4. What type of microenterprise can you start?
5. What incentives do you have to make money?

Don't Forget the Activity Workbook!

Visit **TuttleTwins.com/MarketWorkbook** to download the PDF and provide your children with all sorts of activities to reinforce the lessons they learned in the book!